Your Body

Babies

Anna Sandeman

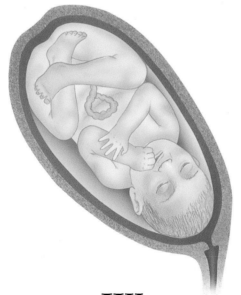

W
FRANKLIN WATTS
LONDON • SYDNEY

New edition published in 2002
© Aladdin Books Ltd 2002
Designed and produced by
Aladdin Books Ltd
28 Percy Street
London W1T 2BZ

*First published in
Great Britain in 2002 by*
Franklin Watts
96 Leonard Street
London EC2A 4XD
Original edition published by
Franklin Watts in 1996

Design: David West Children's Book Design
Designer: Edward Simkins
Illustrator: Ian Thompson
Picture Research: Brooks Krikler Research
Consultants: Dr R Levene MB.BS, DCH, DRCOG
Jan Bastoncino Dip. Ed., teacher of biology and science to 5-12 year-olds

ISBN 0-7496-4828-7

Printed in U.A.E.

Photocredits: Abbreviations: t-top, m-middle, b-bottom, r-right, l-left. All the pictures in this book were taken by Roger Vlitos apart from the pictures on the following pages: 6-7m: Frank Spooner Pictures; 8-9m, 12tl, 12-13m, 13, 14tl, 14-15m, 18t, 29r: Science Photo Library

Contents

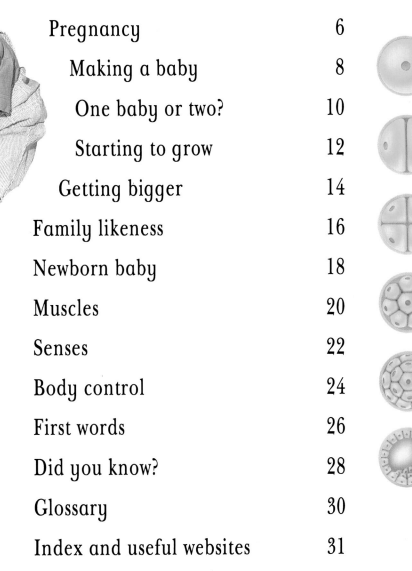

Pregnancy

Can you remember being a baby – when you couldn't walk, talk, or even sit up? Doesn't it seem like a long time ago?

Most animals develop and grow much quicker than humans. A lamb or foal struggles to its feet minutes after it has been born. Both are able to look after themselves within a few weeks. A human baby will probably not walk without help until after its first birthday and is not expected to take care of itself for at least 16 years.

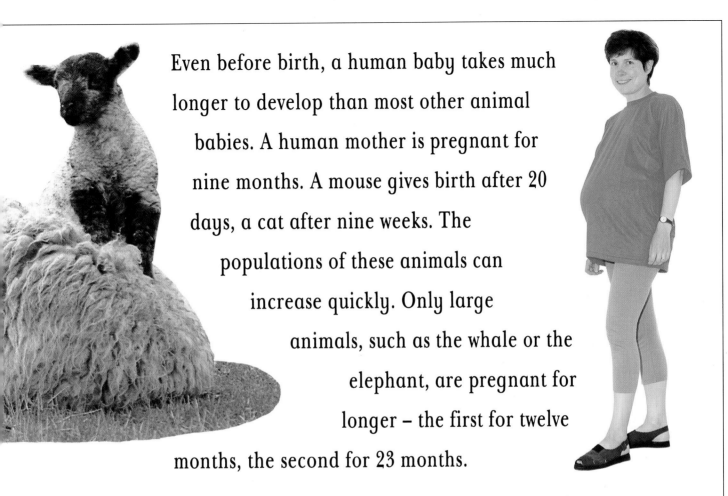

Even before birth, a human baby takes much longer to develop than most other animal babies. A human mother is pregnant for nine months. A mouse gives birth after 20 days, a cat after nine weeks. The populations of these animals can increase quickly. Only large animals, such as the whale or the elephant, are pregnant for longer – the first for twelve months, the second for 23 months.

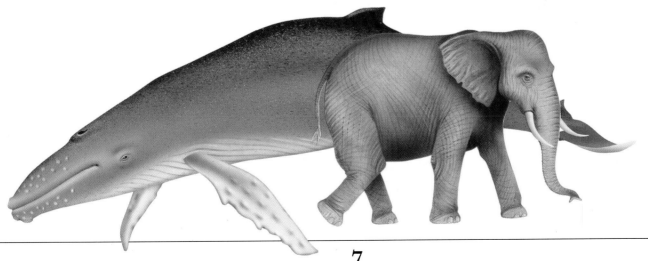

Making a baby

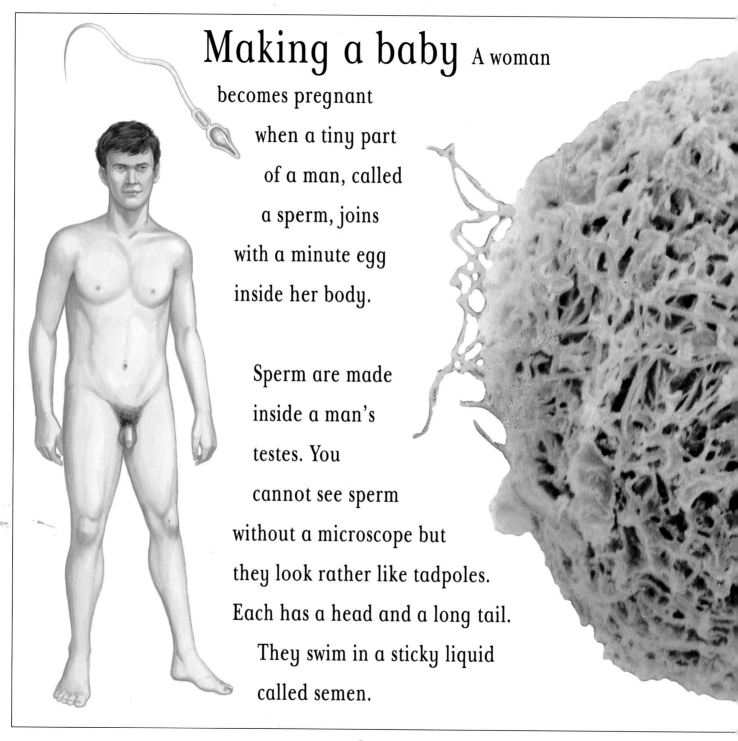

A woman becomes pregnant when a tiny part of a man, called a sperm, joins with a minute egg inside her body.

Sperm are made inside a man's testes. You cannot see sperm without a microscope but they look rather like tadpoles. Each has a head and a long tail. They swim in a sticky liquid called semen.

When a man and a woman want to show their love for each other, the man's penis becomes hard so that it can enter an opening in the woman's body, called the vagina.

Sperm and semen are then squirted through the man's penis into the vagina. From here the sperm swim upwards in their search for an egg.

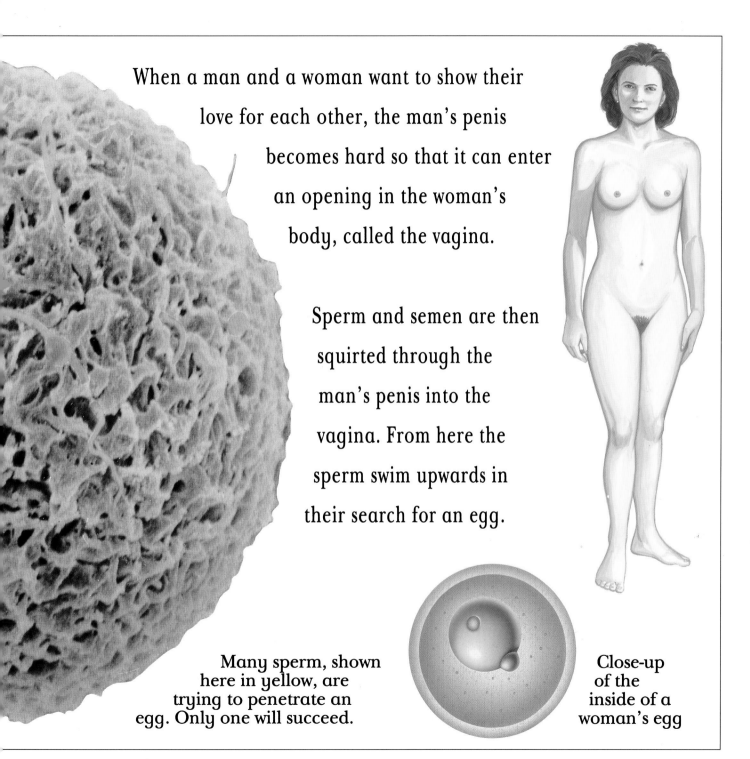

Many sperm, shown here in yellow, are trying to penetrate an egg. Only one will succeed.

Close-up of the inside of a woman's egg

One baby or two?

A fertilised egg divides to form one baby.

A woman's eggs are stored in her ovaries. Every month an egg leaves an ovary to travel down one of two fallopian tubes leading to the uterus. If it meets and joins with a sperm, the egg is fertilised. The fertilised egg is now an embryo. This is the beginning of the baby which will be born nine months later.

A fertilised egg splits into two cells. These two cells divide again and again to form a ball of cells. The ball of cells travels on to the uterus where it settles into the soft lining.

Fallopian tube

An egg is fertilised by a sperm.

Ovary

The embryo embeds.

Vagina

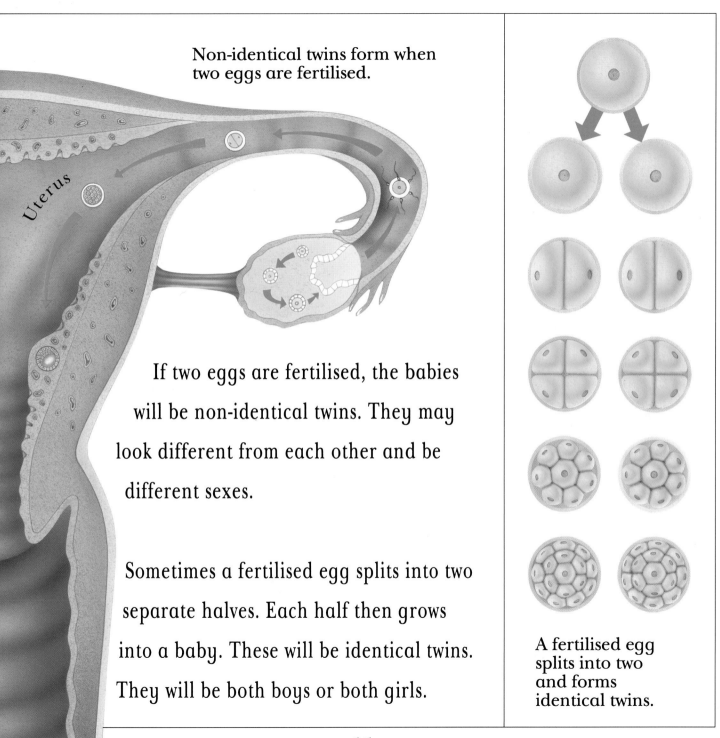

Non-identical twins form when two eggs are fertilised.

Uterus

If two eggs are fertilised, the babies will be non-identical twins. They may look different from each other and be different sexes.

Sometimes a fertilised egg splits into two separate halves. Each half then grows into a baby. These will be identical twins. They will be both boys or both girls.

A fertilised egg splits into two and forms identical twins.

Starting to grow

An embryo at 30 days

Inside the uterus, the cells grow rapidly. They quickly begin to take the shape of a head and backbone. By day 25 the heart is beating, even though the baby is only small – about the size of a baked bean.

By week eight, the baby is 25 millimetres long. Although it is small it already has arms and legs, fingers and toes. It also has the beginnings of a mouth and a nose.

An embryo at eight weeks

12

The baby lives inside a kind of bag filled with liquid. This protects the baby against any bumps and stops the baby becoming too hot or too cold.

The baby is fed by its mother. The food comes in tiny particles, called nutrients. These pass from the mother's blood into a tube, called the umbilical cord, and then into the baby. Look at your tummy button and you will see where your umbilical cord once grew. After birth, the baby no longer needs its umbilical cord so it dries up and drops off.

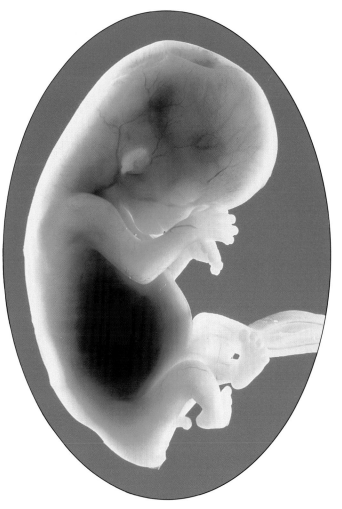

An embryo at eleven weeks

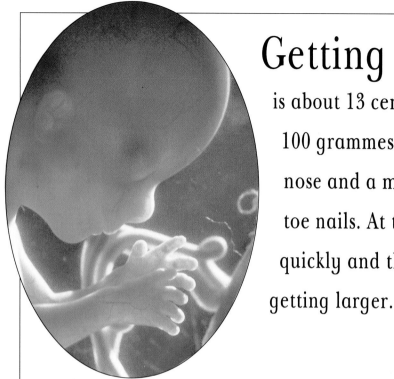

Getting bigger

At 16 weeks the baby is about 13 centimetres long and weighs less than 100 grammes. It has developed eyes, ears, a nose and a mouth as well as finger and toe nails. At this stage the baby grows quickly and the mother's tummy is getting larger.

An embryo at 20 weeks

The embryo at 16 weeks is developing rapidly.

At 20 weeks the mother can feel the baby kicking as it grows and its muscles get stronger. The baby can hear, swallow and suck its thumb. It is beginning to recognise its mother's voice. Some babies even get hiccups!

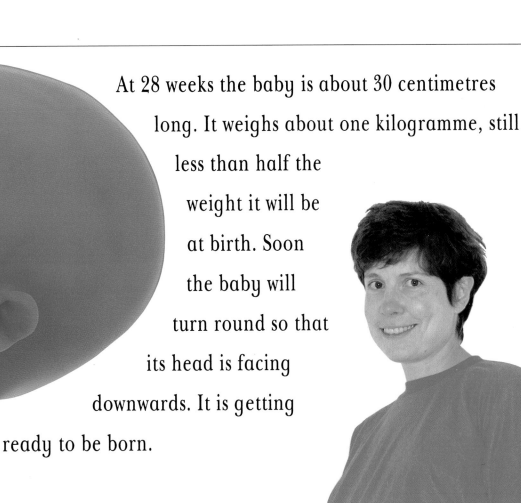

At 28 weeks the baby is about 30 centimetres long. It weighs about one kilogramme, still less than half the weight it will be at birth. Soon the baby will turn round so that its head is facing downwards. It is getting ready to be born.

At 36 weeks the baby's lungs are fully formed. If it were born now, it would be able to breathe on its own. The baby goes on putting on weight. When it is born at around 40 weeks it will be about 50 centimetres long and weigh about three and a half kilogrammes.

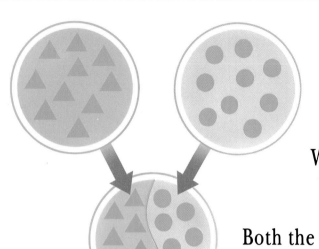

Family likeness

When a baby is born, friends and relatives often say that it looks like its mum or dad. Why?

Both the sperm from the dad, and the egg from the mum, which join up to start a baby, carry their own kind of body pattern. When the egg is fertilised, the two patterns mix together to make a new pattern. This new pattern becomes the body plan for the baby.

Look at this photo of an eight year-old and his parents. Who does the boy look more like?

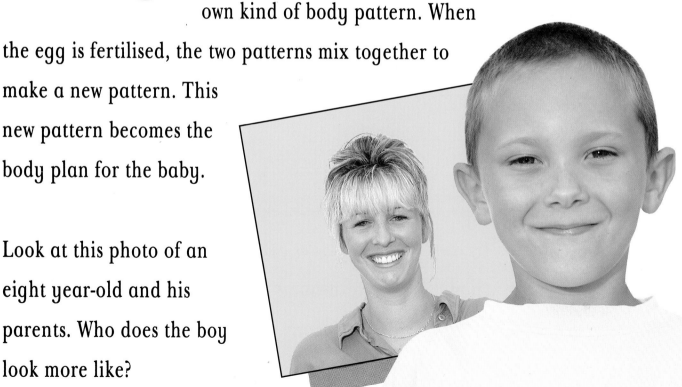

16

The patterns that a mother and father pass on to their baby are made up of the patterns given to them by their own parents. This means that a baby may also look a little like its grandparents.

Ask if you can use photos of your family to make a family tree. Look at eyes, noses and mouths to see which are most like yours. Look at your brothers and sisters too. How are they like you?

Newborn baby

A baby grows most quickly before it is born. After birth, growth is slower. By the end of its first year, it is about three times its birth weight.

As a baby grows, it changes shape. A newborn baby looks very different from you. Although its head is big – about a quarter of the length of its body – its arms reach down only to its hips. Measure the length of your head and arms compared with the rest of you.

Four months

One year

Three years

Look at the pictures below to see how a child's body changes between birth and the age of twelve. What do you notice?

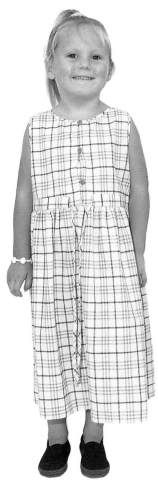

Six years

Ten years

Twelve years

Muscles

Unlike most animals, a newborn baby is almost completely helpless. It can't walk, talk, sit or even lift its head. Its muscles are too weak. Almost all it can do is cry – very loudly.

But from the moment of birth, a baby starts exercising. It waves its arms about and kicks its legs to make its muscles stronger. At this stage, the baby has no control over its movements so it may hit itself in the face by mistake.

Gradually babies learn to use other muscles. By the age of three months, most babies are trying to prop themselves up on their forearms.

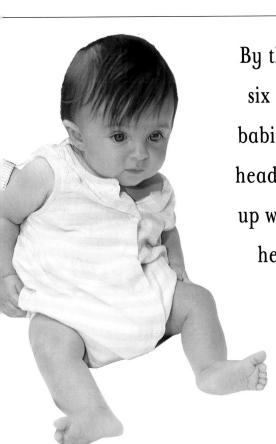

By the age of five or six months most babies can hold their heads up and can sit up with some help.

By eight months, they can sit up without help. At nine months, many babies have learned to crawl.

By eleven months they can walk upright if someone holds their hands, and by their first birthday they may have taken their first step alone.

Senses

Although newborn babies can't move much, they can see, hear, taste, smell and feel things around them.

At first babies can only clearly see things which are very close. When a baby is four weeks old, it watches its mother's face closely as she speaks.

Even very young babies are startled by sudden loud noises. They may blink, cry, fling their arms up, or lie quiet.

Babies are soothed by soft rhythmic sounds. Lullabies, or even a clock ticking may send them to sleep.

Babies have a strong sense of taste and can suck very hard. At first they live just on milk, which they suck from their mother or from a feeding bottle. When they are between three and six months old, they are usually given their first solid food. Most babies quickly make it clear which foods they like and which they don't.

Babies have a sense of smell, too. They even recognise their mothers by their smell.

Crying babies often calm down if they are picked up and cuddled.

Body control

Slowly babies learn to control different parts of their body. At three months they can hold a rattle for a few seconds. At five months, they can grab a nearby toy with two hands. At six or seven months, they can feed themselves with a biscuit and help to hold a spoon while eating.

They now reach for a toy with one hand.

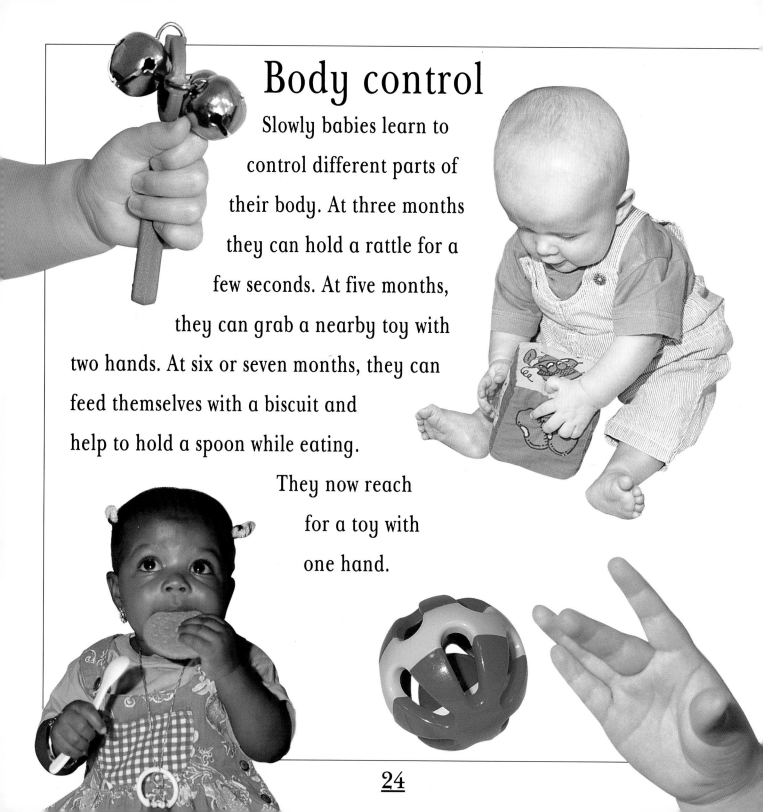

A month or two later, most babies can hold a toy brick in each hand. They turn the bricks around to feel their shape and enjoy banging them on the table.

At ten months, they can bring their thumb and finger together to pick up much smaller objects, such as a piece of string or a pea, and move them carefully from one place to another.

By 18 months they will usually have learned to pile bricks on top of each other or to push objects along the floor with their hands.

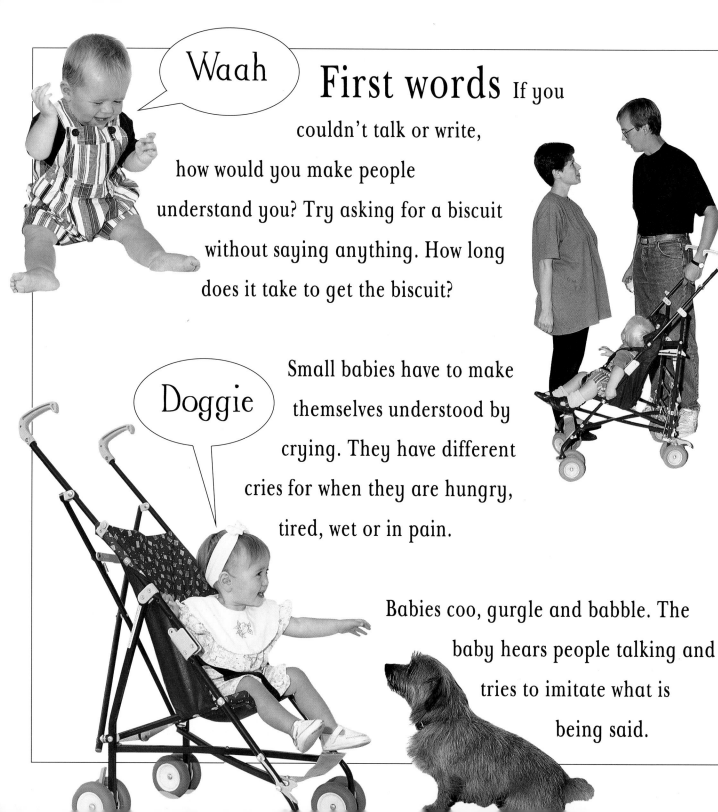

Waah

First words

If you couldn't talk or write, how would you make people understand you? Try asking for a biscuit without saying anything. How long does it take to get the biscuit?

Doggie

Small babies have to make themselves understood by crying. They have different cries for when they are hungry, tired, wet or in pain.

Babies coo, gurgle and babble. The baby hears people talking and tries to imitate what is being said.

Towards the end of a baby's first year, a baby often says its first proper words, such as Mummy, cup or spoon. In its second year, the baby starts to add words to these names – for example,

"Where Teddy?", "Nice doggie".

By the beginning of their third year most babies know enough words to make themselves understood. They can walk and are getting better at making their bodies do what they want. Some are even out of nappies! They are no longer babies; they have become toddlers.

Did you know?

...that a newborn baby's brain is one quarter the weight of an adult's brain, even though an adult is twenty times heavier than a baby?

...that a woman in Russia gave birth to a total of 69 children? She had 16 pairs of twins, seven sets of triplets and four sets of quadruplets.

...that more boys are born than girls? Most babies are born between April and July.

...that if you hold a newborn baby upright, with its feet on the floor, it will try to take steps?

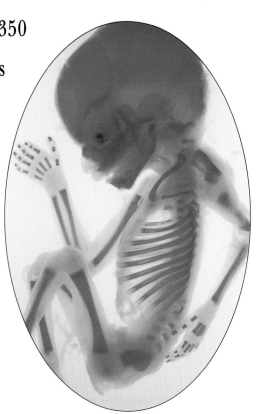

...that a baby has about 350 bones in its body – that's about 150 more than a grown-up?

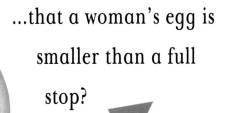

...that a woman's egg is smaller than a full stop?

Glossary

Egg – The female sex cell produced by the ovaries

Ovaries – The female organs that produce eggs

Fertilisation – The process by which a female egg and male sperm join to develop into a new baby

Pregnancy – The development of a young animal inside the uterus

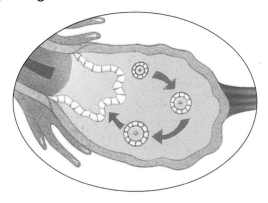

Sperm – The male sex cell produced by the testes

Uterus – The female organ in which the baby develops until it is born

Index

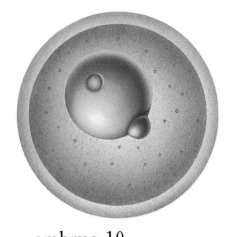

Interested in getting more information on your body and health?

Check out these great websites:

www.kidshealth.org

www.bbc.co.uk/health/kids

CONTENTS

Words in **bold** can be found in the Glossary on page 22.

Bees on the farm

Do you know where **honey** and **beeswax** come from? They are both made by busy, buzzing honeybees.

Honeybees are **insects**. They live in places where there are lots of flowers. Farmers and gardeners like bees because they carry **pollen** from one flower to another. This helps the flowers to make seeds.

4

Down on the Farm

BEES

Sally Morgan

QED Publishing

Written by Sally Morgan
Designed by Tara Frese
Editor Corrine Ochiltree
Picture Researcher Nic Dean
Illustrations by Chris Davidson

Publisher Steve Evans
Creative Director Zeta Davies
Senior Editor Hannah Ray

Printed and bound in China

Picture credits

Key: t = top, b = bottom, c = centre,
l = left, r = right, fc = front cover, bc = back cover

Alamy / The Photolibrary, Wales 15/ terry harris just greece photo library 18 cb / Israel Images 19; **Ardea** / Brian Bevan 4 tl / cr: John Mason 10 cr, 17 tr; **The Art Archive** / Dagli Orti 18 tr; **Beetography.com** / Zachary Huang 17 bl; **Corbis** / Bichon,photocuisine 4 br / Michael Pole 11; **Ecoscene** / Robert Pickett title page / Martin Beames 9 / Stuart Baines 14; **FLPA** / Nick Spurling 5 / Nigel Cattlin fc, 8 tl / Michael Durham 13; **Getty Images** / Frank Greenaway, Dorling Kindersley 6 / Steve Hopkin/Taxi 7 / Terje Rakke, The Image Bank 10 cb / Stockfood bc; **NHPA** / Stephen Dalton 8 br / Martin Harvey 16; **Science Photo Library** Dr. Jeremy Burgess 12.

Beekeepers keep their bees in beehives, like these.

Bees live together in groups called **colonies**. **Beekeepers** are people who look after bees. They build a **hive** for the bees to live in. Most beekeepers look after one or two hives, but some look after many more.

5

Bees from top to tail

There are three types of honeybee that live in a hive. Most are **worker bees**. These are the bees you see buzzing between flowers. A worker bee has a hairy body around 1–1.5cm long. They have two pairs of see-through wings and an orange and black striped body.

Wings

Hairy body

Eye

Sting

Legs

Antenna

This large queen bee is surrounded by worker bees.

FARM FACT
A honeybee can sting. However, once it has used its sting, the bee dies.

Height of a six-year-old child   Height of a beehive

The largest bee in a hive is the **queen** bee. There is only one queen bee in each hive and she is in charge. Male honeybees are called **drones**. There are hundreds of drones living in each hive.

7

It's a bee's life...

The queen bee lays her eggs in the hive. After three days, an egg hatches into a **larva**. The larva is white and has no wings. Worker bees feed the larva with bee bread. This is a mixture of honey and pollen.

Larvae look a bit like wiggly maggots.

After four days, the larva turns into a **pupa**. It stops moving while its body changes into an adult bee.

This baby bee used to be a larva.

Some larvae are given special food to eat, called royal jelly. The worker bees make it in their mouths. Larvae who are fed royal jelly turn into new queens.

Most worker bees live for about six to seven weeks. Drones live for about two months. A queen bee can live for up to two years.

9

Flower friends

Each day, honeybees leave the hive and fly around looking for flowers. They drink the sugary **nectar** made by many flowers.

Flowers produce pollen, too. This looks like yellow dust. Bees put the pollen into special baskets on their legs. They then take the pollen and nectar back to their hive.

This honeybee has collected lots of pollen in its leg basket.

10

FARM FACT
Bees carry the nectar they collect in a special nectar stomach. They have to visit as many as 1500 flowers to fill their honey stomach.

Bees are very helpful little insects because they help to make flowers grow. They carry pollen from one flower to another. This is important because the pollen is needed by the flowers to make their seeds, from which new flowers grow.

Yummy honey

Worker bees chew the nectar and pollen to make it into honey. Honey is very sweet because it is made up of sugar. Bees eat some honey and beekeepers collect the rest. It is strained to remove any beeswax and put into jars to sell.

As much as 70kg of honey can be collected from one hive in a year. That's about the same weight as a grown-up man!

This beekeeper is removing a comb from the hive.

12

FARM FACT
Honey can be used to treat wounds. It stops germs getting into the wound and helps it to heal more quickly.

Honey varies in colour from almost black to white. It can have a strong or a mild taste. It all depends on the types of flowers the bees have visited. Honey made from heather flowers has a smoky taste.

Living in a hive

As many as 50 000 honeybees may live in a hive at a time. That's a lot of bees! Inside the hive, the bees use beeswax to build a **comb**. Each comb is made up of thousands of tiny, six-sided holes, called cells.

FARM FACT
People use beeswax to make candles and furniture polish. Some dental floss is dipped in beeswax so that the floss slides easily between teeth.

When they check their hives, beekeepers wear special clothes so they do not get stung.

In summer, the beekeepers move the hives so the bees have lots of flowers to visit. At the end of summer, they remove some of the combs to collect the honey that has been stored inside. In winter months, when there are few flowers, the beekeepers feed the bees a sugary food, called candy.

15

Bees around the world

KILLER HONEYBEES

The Africanized honeybee is a cross between the honeybee from Europe and the African honeybee. It is found in South America. It has been nicknamed the killer bee because it is a fierce bee that will chase a person more than 100m to sting them. Run!

16

GIANT HONEYBEE

This wild bee is found in Asia and grows up to 15mm long. It makes its nest in trees and on cliffs. Beekeepers don't keep it because it is not very friendly. It will sting a person without reason.

DWARF HONEYBEE

This mini bee is only 8mm long. That's tiny! It lives in southern parts of Asia and is a wild type of bee. Instead of living in a hive, this honeybee attaches its combs to tree branches.

17

Bee customs

ANCIENT EGYPT

Honey was very valuable in Ancient Egypt. It was used like money. One hundred pots of honey were enough to buy an ox or a donkey.

GREECE

In Greece it used to be **traditional** for a bride to dip her finger into a pot of honey and make a sign of the cross before entering her new home. People believed it would bring the bride good luck.

18

ALL OVER THE WORLD

In many parts of the world, honey is part of the Jewish New Year celebrations. Part of the celebration involves dipping slices of apple into honey. This brings good luck for the coming year.

19

Make a buzzy bee

Making your own honeybee is great fun and very easy. All you need is an egg box, scissors, masking tape, paints and paintbrush, pipe cleaners, glue, sticky tape and a plant stick.

1 Cut out two egg shapes from the egg box and stick them together with tape to make an oval shape.

2 Paint the body of the bee. Don't forget that bees have stripy bodies!

3 Cut out a small circle from the egg box and stick it on the front of your bee to make the head. Use your paints to paint on big, boggly eyes.

4 Cut short lengths of pipe cleaner. Stick them onto your bee to make legs and antennae. Bend two more pipe cleaners to make wings, and stick them onto your bee.

5 Make a small hole in the underside of the bee and push the stick into it. Pop your bee in a vase of flowers.

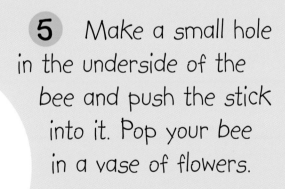

21

Glossary and Index

antenna (plural antennae)   feelers on an insect's body that it uses to touch and feel things

beekeeper   a person who looks after bees

beeswax   a waxy substance made by bees

colonies   large groups of bees that live together

comb   a place where honeybees store honey in a beehive

drone   the name given to a male honeybee

hive   the place where honeybees live

honey   a sugary substance made by bees

insects   small animals with six legs and wings

larva (plural larvae)   the name given to the young of an insect. A larva hatches from an egg

nectar   the sugary liquid made by some flowers

pollen   the yellow 'dust' made by a flower

pupa   the stage in the life of an insect in which the body of the larva changes into the adult insect

queen   the female honeybee that lays eggs

traditional   a custom or way of doing something that is passed from parent to child

worker bees   a type of bee that lives in the hive and collects nectar and pollen from flowers

23

Ideas for teachers and parents

- Watch honeybees at work in a garden or park. Make a note of the flowers the bees visit. Watch how the bees work their way around a flower. Take care that the children do not get too close to the bees, so they do not get stung!

- Look for some interesting recipes that use honey. Make them with the children, then see what they taste like.

- Ask a local beekeeper if it is possible to see inside a hive. Often, local beekeeper associations have open days for members of the public.

- Make a collage of honeybees. Take a large piece of white paper and draw outlines of bees on it, along with some flowers. Look through old magazines and cut out any pictures of bees and flowers. Stick these on the outline to make a colourful collage.

- Make a wordsearch using the bee-related vocabulary in this book.

- Encourage the children to think up jokes and stories about bees. See if they can write a poem or a short story about a honeybee.

- Carry out a simple experiment to see which colours bees prefer. Place three small circles of coloured card (red, yellow and blue) on the ground near a flowerbed and place a little sugar water in the middle of each circle. Stand back and watch which colour of card the bees prefer.

- There are many different types of honey on sale in the shops. Ask the children to look at the labels to see what type of flowers were used by the bees to make their honey. Some are made by bees visiting one type of flower, for example, heather or lavender. It is also possible to buy honey made by rainforest bees. Buy a couple of the different types of honey and do a taste test with the children.

PLEASE NOTE
- Check that each child does not have any food intolerances
  before carrying out the honey recipes and the taste test.

24